The Rascher Collection
SOLOS FROM THE REPERTOIRE OF *Sigurd Rascher*
for E♭ Alto Saxophone and Piano

The Carnival of Venice

Arranged by
GLASER-RASCHER

ITALIAN MELODY

5

Più mosso

cresc.

f stacc.

simile

accel.

ff

ff

8

Slap tongue

a tempo

Gavotte

Arranged by
BREHME-RASCHER

PADRE MARTINI

Sonata No. 3

Arranged by
SIGURD RASCHER

G. F. HANDEL

Ⓔ

Largo

The Rascher Collection
SOLOS FROM THE REPERTOIRE OF *Sigurd Rascher*
for Eb Alto Saxophone and Piano

The Carnival of Venice

Arranged by
GLASER-RASCHER

ITALIAN MELODY

E♭ ALTO SAXOPHONE

Gavotte

Arranged by
BREHME-RASCHER

PADRE MARTIN

Eb ALTO SAXOPHONE

Allegro moderato

Sonata No. 3

Arranged by
SIGURD RASCHER

G. F. HANDEL

E♭ Alto Saxophone

Allegro

Allegro

Prelude to Cantata No. 12
(WEINEN, KLAGEN, SORGEN, ZAGEN)

Arranged by
SIGURD RASCHER

J. S. BACH

Eb ALTO SAXOPHONE

Adagio assai

Prelude to Cantata No. 156
(ICH STEH'MIT EINEM FUSS IM GRABE)

Arranged by
SIGURD RASCHER

J. S. BACH

E♭ ALTO SAXOPHONE

Rigaudon

Arranged by
BREHME-RASCHER

JEAN PHILIPPE RAMEAU

Eb ALTO SAXOPHONE

Variations on a Gavotte by Corelli

Arranged by
GLASER-RASCHER

E♭ Alto Saxophone

Eb Alto Saxophone

Eb **Alto Saxophone**

chappell/intersong ⊕

music group—usa

Exclusively Distributed By

HAL•LEONARD®
CORPORATION

7777 W. Bluemound Rd. P.O. Box 13819 Milwaukee, WI 53213

HL0034780

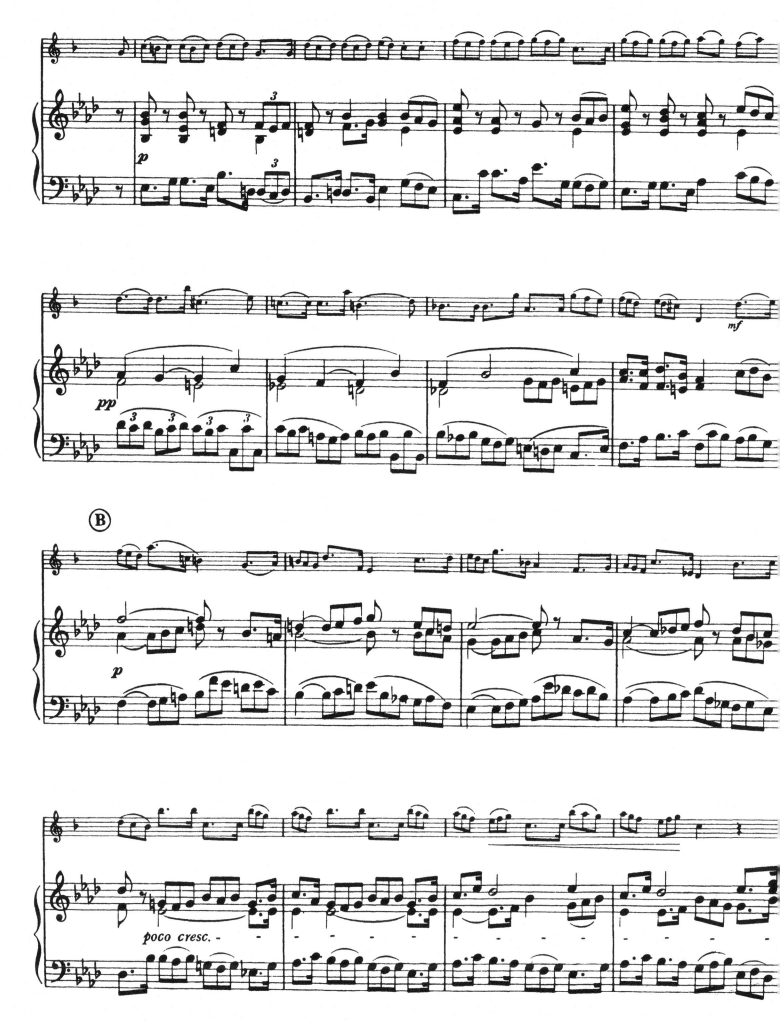

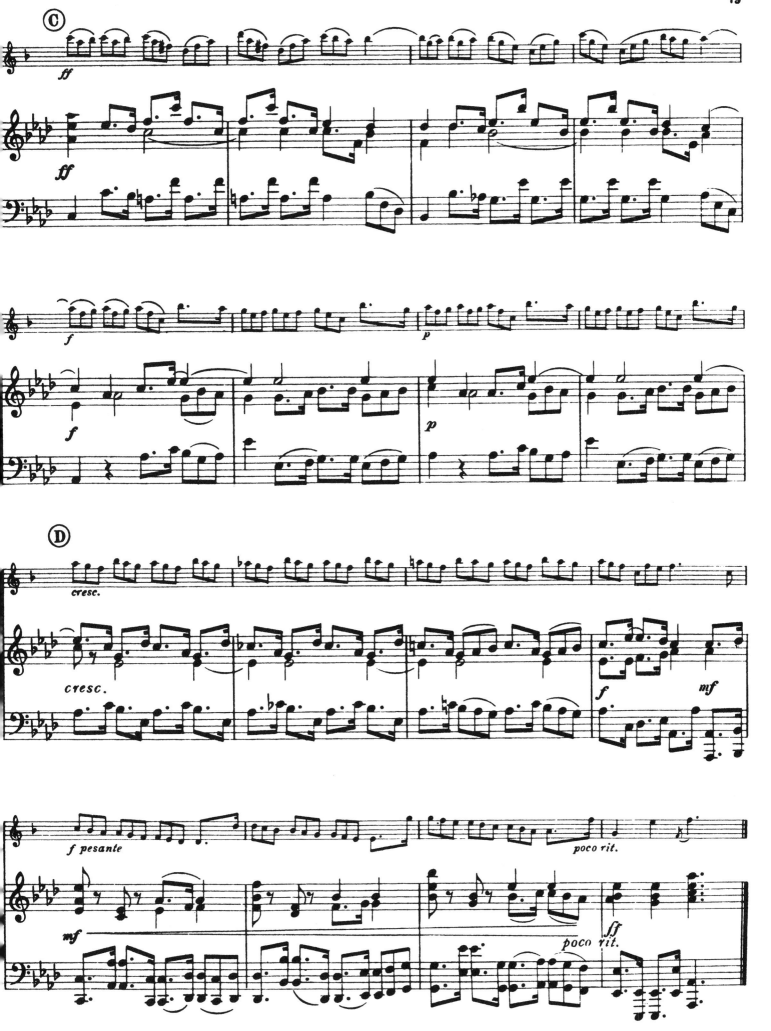

Prelude to Cantata No. 12
(WEINEN, KLAGEN, SORGEN, ZAGEN)

Arranged by
SIGURD RASCHER

J. S. BACH

Prelude to Cantata No. 156
(ICH STEH' MIT EINEM FUSS IM GRABE)

Arranged by
SIGURD RASCHER

J. S. BACH

Rigaudon

Arranged by
BREHME-RASCHER

JEAN PHILIPPE RAMEAU

Variations on a Gavotte by Corelli

Arranged by
GLASER-RASCHER

Var. II

Var. III

Poco andante

Var. IV

Var. VI
Allegro